Wild animals

Les animaux sauvages

lezanee*mo* so-*vajsh*

Illustrated by Clare Beaton

Illustré par Clare Beaton

b small publishing

hippopotamus

l'hippopotame

leepo-pot*am*

elephant

l'éléphant

lellay-*foh*

lion

le lion

ler lee-*oh*

polar bear

l'ours blanc

loo-rss bloh

tiger

le tigre

ler teegr'

monkey

le singe

ler sanjsh

zebra

le zèbre

ler zair-br'

crocodile

le crocodile

ler croco*deel*

kangaroo

le kangourou

ler kongoo-*roo*

giraffe

la girafe

lah shee*raff*

snake

le serpent

ler sair-*poh*

A simple guide to pronouncing the French words

- Read this guide as naturally as possible, as if it were standard British English.
- Put stress on the letters in *italics* e.g. ler sair-*poh*
- Don't roll the r at the end of the word, e.g. in the French word le (the): ler.

l'hippopotame	leepo-po*tam*	**hippopotamus**
l'éléphant	lellay-*foh*	**elephant**
le lion	ler lee-*oh*	**lion**
l'ours blanc	loo-rss bloh	**polar bear**
le tigre	ler teegr'	**tiger**
le singe	ler sanjsh	**monkey**
le zèbre	ler zair-br'	**zebra**
le crocodile	ler croco*deel*	**crocodile**
le kangourou	ler kongoo-*roo*	**kangaroo**
la girafe	lah shee*raff*	**giraffe**
le serpent	ler sair-*poh*	**snake**

Published by b small publishing, Pinewood, 3a Coombe Ridings, Kingston upon Thames, Surrey KT2 7JT.
www.bsmall.co.uk
© b small publishing, 2002
1 2 3 4 5
Design: *Lone Morton*   Editorial: *Catherine Bruzzone* and *Susan Martineau* Production: *Louise Millar* and *Madeleine Ehm*
French adviser: *Claudine Bharadia*
Colour reproduction: Vimnice Printing Press Co. Ltd., Hong Kong.   Printed in Hong Kong by Wing King Tong Co. Ltd.
ISBN 1 902915 69 0
British Library Cataloguing-in-Publication Data.
A catalogue record for this book is available from the British Library.